CHARLES DICKENS'S

The Black Veil

Peter Leigh

Published in association with The Basic Skills Agency

Hodder & Stoughton

A MEMBER OF THE HODDER HEADLINE GROUP

Acknowledgements
Cover: Paul Cemmick
Illustrations: Jim Eldridge
Photograph: Hulton Getty

Every effort has been made to trace copyright holders of material reproduced in this book. Any rights not acknowledged will be acknowledged in subsequent printings if notice is given to the publisher.

Orders; please contact Bookpoint Ltd, 39 Milton Park, Abingdon, Oxon OX14 4TD. Telephone: (44) 01235 400414, Fax: (44) 01235 400454. Lines are open from 9.00–6.00, Monday to Saturday, with a 24 hour message answering service.
Email address: orders@bookpoint.co.uk

British Library Cataloguing in Publication Data
A catalogue record for this title is available from the British Library

ISBN 0 340 77466 5

First published 2000
Impression number 10 9 8 7 6 5 4 3 2 1
Year   2005 2004 2003 2002 2001 2000

Typeset by GreenGate Publishing Services, Tonbridge, Kent.
Printed in Great Britain for Hodder and Stoughton Educational, a division of Hodder Headline Plc, 338 Euston Road, London NW1 3BH, by Redwood Books, Trowbridge, Wilts

About the author

Charles Dickens was born in 1812,
and died in 1870.

He is still one of our most popular writers.
Films and television series are often
made from his stories.

About the story

This is one of Dickens's first stories.
It shows why he became so popular.

It is about ordinary people – even criminals –
and the tragedies in their lives.
There is a young doctor
who is trying to make his way in the world,
and a strange and unhappy woman.

I

One winter's evening a long time ago,
a young doctor was sitting by the fire
in his surgery.

Outside it was wet and cold.
He could hear the rain
pattering against the window,
and the wind rumbling in the chimney.

The young doctor was worried.
He had just begun his medical practice,
and so far he had no patients.
He wanted to get married,
but how could he afford it
if he had no patients?
When would the first one come?

But the fire was bright and cheerful,
and although he was worried,
he began to doze.

He was woken by a knock at the door.
It was very late.
Was this his first patient?

He could see a tall figure
through the glass door.
It was a woman.
She was dressed all in black.
She wore a black shawl round her head
and a thick black veil over her face.

The young doctor jumped up
and opened the door.

'Do you want to see me?' he said.

The figure nodded her head slightly.

'Please come in,' said the doctor.

The figure moved forward slowly.
As she came into the light from the fire
the doctor could see
the bottom of her black dress.
It was soaking wet with rain and mud.

'You are very wet,' said the doctor.

'I am,' said the stranger.
Her voice was full of pain.

'Are you ill?' said the doctor.

'I am,' she replied.
'Very ill. Not in my body, but in my mind.
If my body were ill
I would not be out alone at this hour
or on such a night as this.

But it is not for me
that I have come to you.
It is for another
that I ask your help, sir.
I think I must be mad
to ask you sir.
Nobody can help him now.
It is too late for that.
But my blood runs cold to
think of him lying in
his grave without it.'

A shudder ran through her body.

Her voice was desperate.
It touched the young man's heart.
He was a young doctor
and had not seen much suffering.

'If this person –
the one of whom you speak –
is in the state you describe,
there's not a moment to lose.
I will go with you instantly.
Why did you not come to me before?'

'It would have been useless before –
it is useless even now.'

Think how strange
this must have
seemed to
the doctor – she
wants his help, but
then says
his help would be
useless.

The doctor stared at her.
This was very strange.
He tried to see the expression on her face,
but could see nothing
through the thick black veil.

And then he said gently,
'You are ill.
You are tired and feverish.'

He poured her a glass of water.
'Drink this. Calm yourself,
and then tell me what is wrong with the
patient,
and how long he has been ill.'

The woman raised the glass to her lips
behind the veil,
but then put it down untouched.
She burst into tears.

**seems like the
ravings of fever** –
seems crazy

**I would lay down
my life joyfully** – I
would happily die

'I know,' she said sobbing aloud,
'that what I say to you now,
seems like the ravings of fever
But, although I am not a young woman,
I would lay down my life joyfully
if what I tell you wasn't true.
Tomorrow morning the man I am talking
about
will be beyond help.
And yet tonight,
though he is in deadly peril,
you must not see him,
and you could not help him.'

'I do not understand,'
said the doctor after a pause.
'You say I cannot see this man tonight
when I could help him,
and can only see him tomorrow
when he is beyond help.
Surely if he is dear to you,
why not try to save his life now?'

'God help me!'
said the woman weeping bitterly,
'how can anyone believe me?'

She got up suddenly.

'You will not see him then, sir?'

'I did not say that I would not see him,'
said the doctor, ' but I must warn you,
if the man dies it will be your fault.'

'It will be someone's fault,'
said the woman bitterly.
'Whatever fault is mine
I will answer for it.'

'Well,' said the doctor,
'I will see him in the morning
if you leave me the address.
At what hour can he be seen?'

'Nine,' replied the woman.

'Excuse me for asking,' said the doctor,
'but is he in your care now?'

'He is not!'

'So even if I told you
how to help him through the night,
you could not do it?'

The woman wept bitterly
as she replied, 'I could not!'

at what hour – at
what time

There was no point in any more questions.
The doctor again promised
he would come in the morning.
Then the woman, after leaving the address,
left the surgery in the same mysterious way
as she had entered.

You can imagine the wild thoughts
that rushed through the doctor's head
after she had left.

premonition – a sudden vision of something terrible that is going to happen in the future.

Perhaps she had had a premonition.
He had heard of such cases.
People sometimes knew beforehand
the day, even the exact minute, of their death.
But then he remembered
it was always their own death in such cases.
This woman had spoken of somebody else –
a man.

relented – changed her mind

Perhaps she had planned to murder him
and it was too late to stop.
Perhaps she had relented,
and now wanted to save him.

That was crazy, decided the doctor.
No, his first thought was probably right –
the woman was disturbed, maybe even mad.

But he could not stop thinking about her,
and through a long and sleepless night,
he could not rid his mind of the black veil.

II

Early the next morning
the young doctor set off
for the address the woman had given him.

It was in a dreary place,
little better than a waste land.
The way lay off the main road
over a marshy common.

Remember – at this time, there were very few proper roads or drains, and many people were very poor.

slipshod – with shoes too big for her

As the doctor walked on
he saw only a few broken down cottages,
or a stunted tree, or a pool of stagnant water.
Sometimes a filthy-looking woman
would appear at the door of a dirty house
and empty something into the gutter.
Or she would scream
after a little slipshod girl
carrying a sickly child
nearly as big as herself.
But nothing else was stirring.
A cold damp mist hung over the whole area.

The doctor's spirits sank lower and lower.

After plodding wearily
through the mud and mire,
he finally arrived at the house.

desolate – very lonely and run-down

It was small and low and desolate.
There was one window upstairs
with an old yellow curtain
tightly drawn across it.
There were not other houses around.

He hesitates
because he's a bit
scared.

He had seen the
bodies of people who
had been attacked or
murdered.

The young doctor hesitated,
and walked a few steps past the door.
He could not bring himself to knock.
He knew what could happen
in places like this –
he had seen the evidence in the hospitals.
But then being a young man of strong mind
he stepped briskly back,
and knocked on the door.

There was a low whispering
as if people were talking in hushed voices
and the door slowly opened.

Standing there was a tall, ill-looking man,
with black hair, and a face
as pale and haggard as a corpse.

'Come in, sir,' he said in a low voice.

The doctor did so.
The man closed the door behind him,
and led the way to a small room
at the end of the passage.

'Am I in time?'

'Too soon,' replied the man.

The doctor turned round in surprise,
but the man said,
'If you'll just step in here, sir,
you won't be kept more than five minutes,
I promise.'

The doctor walked into the room.
The man closed the door behind him,
and left him alone.

It was a little cold room,
with only two wooden chairs and a table.
A small fire was burning in the grate,
but all it did was bring out
the dampness in the room.
stole – crept
Water stole down the walls
in long slug-like tracks.
The window, which was broken and patched,
looked out onto a small piece of ground
almost covered with water.
Not a sound was to be heard,
either inside or outside.

The doctor sat down by the fire
and waited for his first patient.

III

After a few minutes
he heard the wheels of a cart
in the street outside.
It stopped outside the house,
and the front door was opened.
There was a low talking
and the sound of shuffling footsteps
along the passage and up the stairs.
It sounded as if two or three men
were carrying a heavy weight
to the room upstairs.

A few seconds later
the stairs creaked again.
The men finished their job
and left the house.

The front door was again closed,
and again there was silence.

Another five minutes passed.
The doctor wondered
whether to get up and look for himself.
But then the door opened
and the woman from last night appeared.

She was dressed exactly as before,
with the same black veil across her face.
Her whole figure seemed wracked with grief.
From beneath the veil
the doctor could hear
the sound of hysterical sobbing.

wracked – tortured

She beckoned him to follow her, and he did so.
She led the way up the stairs
to the front room,
and paused by the door
to let him enter first.

There was a bed,
but the light was so dim
with the curtain pulled tight across the
window,
that he did not see what was on it.
But then the woman rushed past him,
and flung herself on her knees by the
bedside.

motionless – not moving, still

Stretched upon the bed,
closely wrapped in a white sheet,
lay a human form
stiff and motionless.
The head and face were those of a man.
They were uncovered, except for a bandage
which passed over the head and under the chin.
The eyes were closed.
The left arm lay heavily across the bed,
and the woman was holding the hand.

Gently the doctor pushed the woman aside,
and took the hand in his.

'My God!' he said, letting it drop,
'this man is dead!'

The woman started to her feet,
and beat her hands together.

'Oh, don't say so, sir!' she said in a frenzy,
'Don't say so!
I can't bear it,
indeed I can't!
Men have been brought back to life before,
after being given up for lost.
Others have died who might have lived
if they'd have had proper care.
Don't let him lie here, sir,
without one effort to save him.
This very moment his life may be passing
away.
Do try, sir – do, for God's sake!'

While she spoke she hurriedly rubbed
the forehead and the chest of the body,
and beat wildly at the cold hands.

'It is no use,' said the doctor soothingly,
as he took his hand from the man's chest.

'Wait,' he said suddenly.
'Pull back that curtain.'

'Why?' said the woman starting up.
'Pull back that curtain,' he said again,
and rose himself to do it.
But the woman threw herself in front of him.

'Oh sir, have pity on me,' she cried.
'I drew the curtain myself.
Please, sir, if it is of no use,
and he really is dead,
do not – do not expose his body
to other eyes than mine!'

She wants no-one
else to see.

'This man died no natural or easy death,'
said the doctor.
'I must see the body!'

And with that, he tore open the curtain
and let in the full light of day.
He returned to the bedside.

'There has been violence here,' he said,
pointing to the body.

The woman stood up before him,
and ripped off the black veil.
She fixed her eyes upon him.
She was about fifty,
and her face, which had once been beautiful,
was lined with sorrow and pain.
She was deadly pale,
and there was a nervous twitch of her lip.
There was an unnatural fire in her eye,
as if she was about to break down.

'There has been violence here,'
said the doctor again.

'There has!' she replied.

'This man has been murdered!'

'That he has!' cried the woman.
'And I call God to witness it.
He has been pitilessly, inhumanely
murdered!'
'By whom?' said the doctor,
holding the woman by the arm.

'Look at the butcher's marks,
and then ask me!'

The doctor turned his face towards the bed,
and bent over the body
which now lay in the full light of the
window.
The throat was swollen
with a blue, livid mark all around it.

The truth flashed suddenly upon him.

'This man has been hanged!'
he said, turning away with a shudder.

'He has,' replied the woman
with a cold, unmeaning stare.

'Who was he?' asked the doctor.

'My son!' replied the woman,
and fainted at his feet.

pitilessly – without pity;
inhumanely – brutally

livid – dark and angry

unmeaning – vacant, senseless

It was true.
Later the doctor found out the whole truth.
It was an everyday story.
The mother was a widow
without friends or money.
She had given up everything for her son,
and he had grown up
into a life of waste and crime.
This was the result –
his own death by the hangman's hands
and his mother's shame, and incurable
madness.

At this time hanging was a common punishment, even for petty crimes.
His mother was driven mad by shame and grief.

For many years after
when others would have forgotten,
the doctor visited daily the harmless mad
woman,
and soothed her with his kindness.
When she finally died,
her last words were a prayer for his well-
being.

That prayer flew to Heaven
and was heard.
The doctor rose to become
the most famous and honoured doctor of his
time.
But he never once forgot
it was all due to –
the Black Veil.